Tuesday's Child Is Full

in case of emergency press

We are proud to acknowledge the Traditional Owners of country throughout Australia and to recognise their continuing connection to land, waters, and culture.

We pay our respects to their Elders.

We support recognition, reconciliation, and reparation.

Tuesday's Child Is Full

PS Cottier

in case of emergency press
http://www.icoe.com.au
Travancore, Victoria
Australia

Published by **in case of emergency press** 2022

Copyright © PS Cottier 2022

All rights reserved. Without limiting the rights under copyright reserved above, no part of this publication may be reproduced, stored in or introduced into a database and retrieval system or transmitted in any form or any means (electronic, mechanical, photocopying, recording or otherwise) without the prior written permission of both the owner of copyright and the above publishers.

ISBN 978-0-6453751-2-1

Title Page photo **Alex Wigan**
Photo of the author **Geoffrey Dunn**

Foreword

Since 2009, I have maintained a blog called *pscottier.com*. For most of those thirteen years, I have posted an original poem once a week, usually on Tuesdays. For part of this time I was a member of a group, mostly based in Aotearoa New Zealand, committed to posting every Tuesday, and linking with other poets. The Tuesday Poets wound up in 2015, after five years, but the habit of posting poetry once a week has stayed with me. Lapses in posting at my blog are a good indication of either depression or laziness. Or both.

Most agree that the golden age of text-based blogs is well behind us, pushed out by more immediate social media. However, I find there is something valuable in this kind of publication, at once more relaxed and, seemingly, a little more permanent than the frantic communication from which many are never free. A blog provides freedom for the poet to publish what she wants, to experiment and to play. The only costs are time, registering a domain, and, perhaps, paying to have no advertisements appear.

Rereading the thirteen years of posts, I discovered many of the recurrent ideas and preoccupations that have found their way into my poems. Flight is something that appears again and again, jostling with descriptions of land-based animals. Noisy meditations on poetry itself are quite frequent. Nastiness also has its place, as do fantasy creatures. Politics is inevitably imbedded in a number of works, and music is sometimes heard. I have selected poems from the blog and present them here in an order that seems to read well.

In the traditional rhyme, Tuesday's child is full of grace. This selection may not be particularly graceful, but there are ideas and wordplay, and I believe that the works merit a translation from blog to the undeniably more permanent medium of paper. I have not included many of the poems that have previously made that leap, but there are a few as detailed in the following acknowledgements. Some poems have been lightly edited.

PS Cottier

Acknowledgements

'April (is it a haibun?)' is an amalgam of two blog posts from April 2020. The haiku beginning 'Autumn wind' included here was distributed on tear-off posters as part of the Haiku 4 You project during the Poetic City Festival in Canberra, curated by Jacqui Malins

'The canary, the pony and the man' published *Utterly*, Ginninderra Press, 2020

'Currawongs' highly commended in the Ipswich Poetry Feast, 2010 and also published on the competition website. Included in *The Cancellation of Clouds*, Ginninderra Press, 2011. 'Teeth' was also included in this collection.

'Heron's formula' commended in the World Wetlands Day Poetry Prize, Feb 2016.

'Ten-minute prose poem' was written at Au Contraire, the New Zealand Science Fiction convention, 2013, in a poetry workshop facilitated by Tim Jones and Harvey Molloy. The exercise was to write a poem describing a piece of future technology, and to build it or take it apart for the reader.

'We are all working our way up, towards the birds' was highly commended in the Interstellar poetry award, 2015, and published *Quick Bright Things: Poems of Fantasy and Myth*, Picaro Press Imprint, Ginninderra Press, 2016. 'Oppressing the gnomes' was also included in this collection.

Table of contents

Fungi	1
All hail the tip turkey	2
This poem is a birdbath	3
Mouth brooding	4
Currawongs	5
Moderately threatening bird	6
Colonials	7
(haiku 1)	8
April (is it a haibun?)	9
April was the cruellest month	10
Greyhounds' release	11
Do dogs dream of flying?	12
A woman crossed the road	13
No obituary	14
Backyard farms	15
(haiku 2)	16
sequential menu	17
Finite	18
Mango	19
Wattle	20
Heron's formula	21
We are all working our way up, towards the birds	23
Teeth	24
(senryu 1)	25
Even snails	26
Peripheral vision flicker (A poem found at Conflux)	27
A timely monster	28

Remembering those who gathered in 1816 by the shores of Lake Geneva, along with monsters and vampires	29
Mary Shelley's Cookbook	30
Turn away	31
Fernando Pessoa shaves	32
(haiku 3)	34
Just may be	35
(haiku 4)	36
The home for ancient memes	37
Ten-minute prose poem	38
Oppressing the gnomes	39
Seven dwarfs	40
A parachute of avocados	41
The tea-lady's dream, 1970	42
On the sticky retirement of myth	43
Clumsy in love	44
Roll up! Leap through!	45
music notes	46
Jazz	47
Guide to not writing haiku	48
13 words that should be in a poem	49
Perfect words	50
There are five poets in my garden	51
Eighth in a long line of nasty little poems	52
Second in a long series of nasty poems	53
First in a long series of nasty little poems	54
Third in a long series of nasty little poems	55
Outings	56
(haiku 5)	57
(senryu 2)	58

Twenty ways to keep your essentials to hand	59
The poet contemplates the inescapable nature of the class system	60
I remember the lost skirt of Carlton	61
French police cut soles off migrant children's shoes	62
Three first world concerns	63
The canary, the pony, and the man	64
You can't stand outside	65
Malcolm Turnbull's tie	67
Faith took a holiday	68
Limits	70
Ten moments in the life of modern Jesus	72
Except for the cat	73
About the Author	75

Fungi

They are not one nor the other
neither animated beasts
nor sluggish vegetables.
We see them as ambiguous,
but they are what they are,
have no need for categories
to undermine like mulch.
Some have an orange that is limitless.
Ten trillion angelic spores tickle the air.
They join forests with reaching non-fingers.
They are neither sadness nor glee.
Persistent softness breaks down logs.
Some push up after rarest rain—
quaint exclamation reversed,
cap upright but no mere tittle,
and not a little 'i'.
They mouth off.
They are easily mistaken—
or rather, we mistake them,
rejecting our uncertainty.
Poison is just a flicker from food,
kidneys breaking down like wood.
They are not one nor the other—
they have their ways.
Would that we were they.

All hail the tip turkey

Tip turkey works through the plastic—a TROJAN

Tip turkey has no time for posing—he's no STATUE

Tip Turkey is adorned with smears—saucy TOMATO

Tip Turkey cries to the sky—frogs smoke CIGARETTES

Tip turkey smells unpleasant—but not more than a homely TIP

Tip turkey fell from perfect grace—some still call him SACRED

Tip turkey is no pink flamingo—no smiling lawn adorning TIP

Tip turkey is flung at the margins—discarded CIGARETTES

Tip turkey is letting himself go—bald seedy as TOMATO

Tip turkey follows reckless trash—a tributary STATUE

Tip turkey has no hidden surprise—he's no TROJAN

Tip turkey is a common name for *Threskiornis moluccus*, the Australian white ibis. It is also known as the bin chicken. Ungainly on the ground, tip turkeys fly in a beautiful arrow formation. The poem attempts to reflect this.

This poem is a birdbath

and it fills itself with bird
the quick splash of silvereye
the suspicious sip of currawong,
unable to believe in non-carnivorous gift—
looking out for bigger beaks behind the bush.
This poem features no sudden cat, lurking,
a sonnet's volta, waiting to rewrite the tone
from mild celebration to whiskered doom.
The water slops over the rim of
                the poem.

The mess feeds the grass below, as do the birds.
Birds draw no firm distinctions between bath
and toilet. They revel, quietly, and the poem
expresses gratitude, for being, for being merely.

Mouth brooding

In damp mulch, it swallows eggs like knowledge.

In a quiet vocal sac (now choked from croak)

they form into commas, hoping to punctuate

the forest's leafy library of tales. It spits!

Out pops a haiku of wiggle,

a soft finger of amphibian,

pooling into an anthology of puddle.

Seven froglet booklets, sprightly as thoughts,

swim towards their future. Must this language,

this webbed poem, be forever lost?

Currawongs

Weaving nets of strong noise in the air,

the electric weft and warp alarming,

they swoop down, direct as any stare.

They are nobody's favourite bird,

brunching on bright blue wrens

or snacking on smorgasbords

of tenderised olive silvereyes.

They watch us watching them,

estimate our worth, and dismiss us

from their mental menu: *Too big,*

head too tough to spear with beak.

This is why we dislike these

sharp gazed moving funerals.

They don't sing for us, or plume for us,

and reduce us to something at the edge.

Currawongs' natures know no flattery,

offer nothing to our mountainous vanity.

Beyond cute, below eagle's sky-high beauty,

they care only for their meat, song and nest.

They tell us that we are not the centre,

the be-all, the crux; the inarguable best.

Moderately threatening bird

Between budgie and hawk
you flutter your mild wings,
which still cause wee jumps
in heart rate or blood pressure—
more wallaby than pole vault.
You don't pick eyes out
like ravens of ill repute
(though I've always been partial
to those most Victorian birds).
You don't trade messages with the dead,
or lead the undead back to tossed bed
of sea doona, or semen sheet.
Yet you are somewhat disquieting,
with your cleverness beyond our control.
So we clip your wings, and ignore
the unclipped birds flocking in our heads.
Ideas swarm like sparrows
and each one is falling into dread.

Colonials

Angels dancing on pins are nothing to us,
those celestial pricks number thousands,
harpies with harps, slippery butterflies.
We live in millions, simple stars.
A bone slung hammock,
your body transports us
as we rock, divide, and redivide.
Under the curved
frowns of your fingernails,
on the flaky deserts of your head,
we plant our sprawling flag.
Any crevice is our castle, your mouth
a plunge-pool for our disport.
Arise, Sir Realm, Sir Habitat.
King Bacillus is well pleased.

(haiku 1)

persistence of jellyfish

flesh liaisons bloom

sea-flowers have no soul

'sea-flowers...' is from Jules Verne, *20,000 Leagues Under the Sea*

April (is it a haibun?)

How many parrots there are in Canberra, sulphur-crested cockatoos and corellas, with young birds begging to be fed.

The sun was out, and I found myself plainly happy, totally forgetting about coronavirus for a short while. Of course, just for a moment, and soon it was back to skirting around any other walkers and cyclists. I felt almost guilty for feeling so good, thinking about the many older people stuck inside, and the crew of the cruise ship Ruby Princess still confined aboard, and, of course, the people who have died from the virus.

The hundreds of dogs so delighted that their owners are home so much more now have no inkling as to the virus, and I envy them their lack of knowledge.

My mind wagged
my thoughts spaniels
licking the air

We are lucky that we can still get out and stroll around for necessary exercise, and even buy a takeaway coffee, and observe the natural world that reaches right into suburbia. Screeching or smelling.

Autumn wind
white leaves swirling
cockatoos

April was the cruellest month

I miss the pub noise
*S*ociety contracts like a fist
*O*ld people dying in dozens
*L*anguishing/anguishing/wishing
*A*ustralia pulls up the biggest drawbridge
*T*oo many whiskies, no balancing gym
*I*diotic President's bleached tips
*O*nly me and the spoilt dog
*N*ovel coronavirus drags

Greyhounds' release

Let them run—
but run as they would
chasing the wind or their mate
not a screeching curl-tailed baton
flung round the track
in a circular curse.

And let them live—
just as long as greyhounds live
not dispatched for slowness
and spaded into the bush
in a quotidian slaughter
nose to tail, tail to nose.

Do dogs dream of flying?

The paws scrabbling during dreams,
the muffled barks, wrapped in cloud;
could it be they chase sparrows
up beyond tight leash of earth?

How far do their brains stretch,
those companions of smooth aliens,
those interpreters of foreign voice?
They know to find meaty meaning
in nonsensical noise we make,
the complicated sound droppings
we float into blank noseless air.

Why then could dog not look beyond
and dream of wings, of slipped collar
soaring? Little Pegasus of wag,
small brown scented eagle;
scratching blue in basket bliss.

Rainbow of smells is beckoning.

A woman crossed the road

                    when she saw my Staffy
and I wanted to call out she's a honey!
she only bites her food, and she loves
to lie on her back, let the sun delve
into her belly, and when I watch her,
I feel happy, almost as happy as when she
sees me, and her tail wags her body,
but I could not help but feel punctured
by the woman equating this dear dog with
violence, I could not help feeling anger,
and realised she had turned one part of me
into a poor imitation of how she sees Staffies,
for I felt like chasing her, shaking the nonsense out,
out of her head, and instead I reached down,
and patted the keg of a dog that she had spurned
just because dog-she carries a sad history
written by some thoughtless people
upon her plump body and her muscled breed.

She wagged her tail, oblivious.
My lips stretched to a smile.

No obituary

Presented to us in a terrier's mouth,
he squirmed his way back into being
through a tight vice of punctures.

Dinny (the dog's near dinner).
An experimental dish who charmed
with his monomania for grass.

Grass in and grass out,
pelleted, my weed and feed,
my murmuring mower of lawn.

Tonight we return him to grass
and precious green will sprout
from pink, once eager mouth.

No obituary for a guinea pig
that simple vegetarian of soul.
None, that is, save this.

Backyard farms

Corrugations echo with cluck,
the occasional illicit crow,
ear-pecked neighbours pick fights;
shrill voices make 6 a.m. alarms.

Frosted into internal mush,
harder shell of fallen white,
strawberries mimic the avid snails
munching them like Frenchmen.

Orange peel, meat and coffee
strewn on sacred stewing mounds
create decomposition. Disbelief
that she knows so little, cares less.

(haiku 2)

Old green turtle
round mummy in plastic
excess drowning

sequential menu

methane farts
too many cows
thick beefy skies

thick beefy skies
drive for takeout
taste that plastic

taste that plastic
(onion rings)
defenestration

defenestration
gutter wrapper
sea junk flourishes

sea junk flourishes
macturtles sup
second hand meat

second hand meat
too many cows
thick beefy skies

Finite

A limited number of autumns
mulched, or tumbled in a barrel,
spread thin, or just allowed to fall.
The angry man with the blower.
The desperate, toothy rake,
plied like a weapon to hold back
swarming leaves of dragon red.
Carpeting drive and inscribing soil—
the pointed, scarlet letters
of a limited number of autumns.

Mango

Skinned sun bleeds thickest honey,
flesh cubed into soft armadillos.
You whisper of summer, twin ears,
lure us like that other yellow,
the smiling curve of beach.
Lie in a hammock—
canvas forming cocoon—
and eat a mango;
where fruit ends and we start
is hard to say. Peel away
accretions of words and worries—
be stroked by gold to dream.

Wattle

Confetti throws handfuls of self
against ecstatic sky
cheering its union with blue.

This is no watercolour plant.
Each bubble blown is distinct
a life born from Winter's death.

I look at the tree and see God, hear
a choir of yellow lungs, inflated.
But then again, I'm not allergic.

Heron's formula

A lesson in trigonometry,
the white heron forms triangles
with legs as she inches forward
< obtuse, acute, obtuse >
and reeds write the shape's third side,
grass and leg linked by my needy eye.

Each retraction from stillness
seems a matter of regret;
a fall from Greek statue
into hungry, stalking GIF.
Silent as a wish, she moves
towards the modest,
root-dwelling fish.

A split triangle
wedged into head axes down,
teaching the dumb water
a critical formula: working an equation
on softer bodies.

Heron swallows, then cries triumph,
and the noise is the croak
of a thirty-a-day frog
krarkkrarking imperfection—
a broken kaleidoscope of notes—
a pocket full of clashing change.

The breath of the eager teacher
who tried to show me the

dubious wonders of triangles,
to draw them on my brain,
swings into memory
with a scalene sharpness.
Sound conjures smell;
ear and nose separated only
by a stretched vinculum of years.

Angel microbes swarmed
in his every exhalation,
armed with gleeful mallets
for playing smell croquet —
sulphur tapped through nostrils —
blunt, yet sharp and jangling.
He could not know that
he was Alice with stink flamingos;
heroic feathers tickling
before, and after, each own goal.
How could I breathe and think
under such an unnumbered cloud?
A limp fish, I soon failed.

The elegance of herons
undercut by noise;
the perfection of mathematics
negated by disgust.

I paddle off, towards firm ground,
away from the sharp, white assassin,
and the chopped pools of recollection.

We are all working our way up, towards the birds

We are all working our way up, towards the birds.
Outliers like Icarus, 70s pterodactyl hanggliders,
twitchers and breeders of weird coloured parrots:
they have all felt the urge and responded
to the best of their beakless capacities.
But they are not the neo-orno avant-garde.
The egg must come first, before the flight—
putting aside philosophy, that is just true.
So who is nature's true Anna Wintour?
Where is the next Paris to be found?

The catwalk of the world is spiked by echidna.
Platypus pouts there too. (That is hard with a bill.)
These two are the fashion-forward models,
who will soon sprout wings and launch and fly;
it is happening now, as I type and you read.
Placenta will be ditched, like yesterday's rags.
Next year, unaided flight will be de rigueur,
and song will erupt, without instruments,
deep from the gape of seven billion throats.
We are all working our way up, towards the birds.

Teeth

Baby teeth parade in neat lines
proclaiming perfect evenness.
Easy equation in which numerator
and denominator meet and greet
over pink board of lisping tongue.
Gummy foundations for architecture
of white, well-placed tiny bricks.
But the gothic develops quickly.
Dark gaps gape like blind eyes
between crooked slates of ambition.
Tooth grows over tooth, bony excess,
lurking doppelgängers of tusk.
Then mouth exorcises milky ghosts
and settles down to grown-up sense,
grinding out a modest lifetime;
our well-worn, skullful suburb of jaw.

(senryu 1)

camera catches
side-eye and grimace
'say *rictus!*'

Even snails

Peg loves looseness, envies river of sheet,
flowing down from plastic clench of beak.
Milk would carve itself into solidity, escape
sloppy white seascape into certainties of cheese.
Poet would be musician, shed sad bad husks of words,
sprout into airier art, so eary and so letterless.
Sliming through house-heavy dirt,
even snails may dream of wings.

Peripheral vision flicker
(A poem found at Conflux)

That subterranean process
alien or not alien
everyone is pretending
peripheral vision flicker
she can smell if you're sad
more oxygen than carbon
prone to sooting
the aroma of porcelain
observe the strange world!
I was actually swooning
wouldn't send a trunk story
we churn through them
faffing around before
a source of buoyancy
sketchy with world building
arrogant rockstar scientist
no socks in fantasy land
bounce off the person you are
every village is a city
chunky unspeakable matter
just people in an environment
herbivore men
arcane and hideous process
when we have wings
tend not to rhyme
a paisley black hole

Conflux is a science fiction convention held in Canberra.

A timely monster

And if I could drink youth in
through my eyes—a vampire
of glance, lapping it from
perfect blush of skin—
would it be possible not to
drink and rise, leaving years
like a phone lost in cushions?
And yet, and yet...
before my eyes suck, remember
the self-consciousness,
the rash redness of life
before it wrapped itself in time?
To take, and lose a burden,
is to lift another,
cutting into hands or mind,
like an overloaded bag.
So let them pass, and let me yearn
and learn to stop, just here.
I'll sit, and plait kind memory
through this smoked nostalgia of hair.

Remembering those who gathered in 1816 by the shores of Lake Geneva, along with monsters and vampires

We'd all be Byron, if we could;
titled, desired, transgressive.
What wouldn't we all give
to write Mary's monster half as good?
Or to pen Ozymandias,
and find ourselves anthologised,
with the glamour of one who died
as young as PB. There's a bias
towards such as he, or Jimi Hendrix.
Mary Shelley lived a longish life
but many cast her just as the wife
of genius drowned. As if she were thick!
Yes, in our hearts, we opt for glory.
Pity we're all Polidori.

John Polidori was present with the trio of geniuses during the famous stay in 1816. He was Byron's doctor. He wrote the first full length vampire story in English. When published it was attributed to Byron, who denied authorship. The prose in the novel can generously be described as pedestrian.

Mary Shelley's Cookbook

Bind this book
in the skin of man.
Keep your place marked
with fingers,
or tongues to taste
the lineaments.
Take kidneys, lights and liver
and animate the contents
with diseased and wandering imagination.
Forget your sex.
Just write.

'Diseased and wandering imagination' is from an early review of Frankenstein in *The British Critic*. Possibly the first reviewer to realise that the author was female, the writer criticised Shelley for 'forgetting the gentleness of her sex'.

Turn away

Turn away from the night.
Too much freedom is implied.
Trap stars in flags, pin them down,
render them national, bordered,
an angular abacus to figure normality.
Adorn children's essays with thin
gold paper star stickers.
Wonder is juvenilia that we must
grow to despise, jettison
like milk teeth swapped for coin.
Yet those million suns, flickering
light sirens, keep calling, ululating.
Day demands in clear clipped diction
that we make work's timed rituals
the sum of all equations. From such
abbreviation, each star whispers
turn away, turn to me,
turn to me, and turn away.

Fernando Pessoa shaves

—and needless to say, the mirror
has three leaves. So at least
twelve chins require scraping
(for they all go beardless,
or at least, sometimes so)
and one, or four, can't always
leave, to visit the barber.
Eight hands, a lively *polvo*,
attempt to shave straight,
but, let's face it (ha!)
straight is not really
in their repertoire.

It is disconcerting when a man
metamorphoses from Fernando
into Alberto between nose and chin
as one uses a blade as blunt
as omniscience. Little rivers
open up, and flow into each other.
In one mirror-wing, Álvaro bleeds
and in the other, Ricardo winces.
The eight hands become twice twelve
in the trinity of glass.
In the corner of one wing,
see that crack? One, or four,
become a jigsaw, no, a galaxy
of Fernando and his others.

This is the image which one might
or could possibly call true.
The eye of one bends into
chin of the other; a quiet, crazed
Picasso, but with a line less sure.

He had never belonged
to a crowd. Except to himselves.

Fernando Pessoa's main heteronyms included Alberto Caeiro, Álvaro de
Campos and Ricardo Reis. He also wrote as Fernando Pessoa. 'He had never
belonged to a crowd' is from the Preface to *The Book of Disquiet*, by Pessoa (or
Bernando Soares) tr. R. Zenith.

(haiku 3)

Behind the parlour
nail clippings rejoice
castanets

Just may be

Just may be, out there, there's another place
where placentas are the exception,
and green marsupials lie on towels
and listen to the orange surf,
as the unspeakable snags roast on the fire,
and idly glance up to the unraked sky
where the stars like sand tell rumours
of the other, possible places that we call here.

(haiku 4)

Gloves house hunger
moths make gaping mouths
finger tongues speak

The home for ancient memes

Where they can haz cheeseburgers all day
Where jokes of nuking each other from space crack
Where everyone fusses over a grumpy cat
Where the cry of Ermahgerd echoes
Where an overly manly man flexes, endlessly
Where sad hipsters say many things
Where planking takes place every evening
Where the X all the Ys, and Y all the Xs
Where ice buckets become challenging
Where smugshrugs shrug smugly
Where seals have awkward moments
Where they debate the colour of a dress
Where they still Netflix and chill
Where…I'd definitely continue, but
Ain't nobody got time for that

Ten-minute prose poem

My skull peels back like a hairy banana. A hairy banana dusted with a coconut of dandruff, which confettis the floor. Inside I find the familiar lumps: the lobes raised into a fairy ring of concentric bumps. Those brain tits, as Jean calls them.

Pouting against bone
modestly encased in skull
my brain jiggles thought

My fingers locate the zips that hold the sims in place, and slowly—mirror work is always slow—I unzip the first bump nestled like an egg on the top of the brain. I am losing my ability to speak French, you see, and this sim is my language supplement. Rain and tears, dogs and hatred, have been running into each other like a water-colour; or as in the subtle distinctions between air and smoke and sea and ship that we see in Turner's works.

French bleeding meaning
parapluie of sense
springing unwell holes

Easy then, to replace the chip, rezip, and close. Tomorrow the chemist. Dandruff clouds.

Fin.

Oppressing the gnomes

The garden gnomes are downing tools
all over Australia, and whimsy is plummeting.
No more riding snails and pushing barrows,
or fishing for strangely ecstatic cod,
who gape for hooks in a pornography of cute.
The gnomes are turning nasty, attacking
the flamingos who continue to strut —
elegant pink scabs over the quirky lawns.
Gnomes piss on succulents and smear
foul gnome shit on the guinea pigs.
What do we want? they ask the air.
But they don't know what to chant back —
their dissatisfaction is merely existential.
Even their industrial action raises a laugh,
with their crooked green caps slipping,
and their endless pipes twixt ruddy lips.
Their signs are egregiously misspelt.
Nome's R Us is at least legible,
but the kerning is much worse than that,
and the punctuation speaks volumes.
Get back to it, gnomes, I say, imperiously.
Ply those forks, and play that accordion.
I bask in my elevation to exploiter,
swaying in a complacent hammock.
Surly yet amusing, the wee green men obey.
The ringleader rides a frog to the pond,
and casts in his line like a sigh.

Seven dwarfs

1.
Aladdin's café
health foods, humous, saffron
Open Sesame

2.
haiku yakuza
execute punctuation!
killer formalists

3.
If poetry
is the mouth
critics pulling
are needle-mad dentists

4.
Grey ghosts of planes
winding down to Gitmo
cigar smoke blows

5.
Bonsai triffids
cut down to flowerpots
balcony stings

6.
Sun fishing
gravity snags planets
hook bites deep

7.
Manga and cartoon
smooth cheese and wasabi
spreading mayhem

A parachute of avocados

A parachute of avocados, plunging through dipping air;

fifteen seconds to wonder if persimmons would have been a better choice;

five seconds to understand the grounding nature of vegetables;

and you plant yourself, scattered red nasturtium, sprinkled on salad of lawn.

The tea-lady's dream, 1970

No-one wanted tea. I felt my stockings
thickening, darkening. Varicose veins
still wrote Chinese messages,
but sudden trousers held the blue.
My twisted wrist ached, and a warm smell
better than shortbread, browner than treacle
wrapped me in blankets of singing air.
New words jingled in my pocketed ears.
Foreign coins: *crema, doppio, arabica,*
even mugaccino. They sipped and said
You're the city's best barista.
I strained confusion to comprehend.
No-one wanted any tea.

On the sticky retirement of myth

Pegasus got too old
so Bellerophon melted him for glue.
Useless glue; for each pot is full
of feathers. Lovely scrapbooks
are ruined by inconvenient discards,
as grandmothers grow downy beards,
and babies sport Trumpy wigs.
And they fly into the air, too,
the photos, nay, the very books,
and escape into the ether,
to gallivant with feckless clouds.
Never use a famous winged horse,
where a broken legged nag will do.

Clumsy in love

Clumsy wears ugg boots, where others don high heels,
or light reflective slippers of glass. They waltz,
all Straussy and fine in white, with froufrou and swish.
Clumsy stomps. Even his sheepskin words betray him.
He muffles passion in good intention, dags' love
in a brown blanket of nag. Clumsy would be lacy,
suggestive, a slight touch between eyelash and wink.
But his eagerness clutches and grabs, rummages
for a lost gold key of ease. He speaks words
subtle as a losing barracker at three-quarter time,
pie's warm filling dripping onto his mind's feet.
Dreams subsist, nonetheless, in quiet fleecy nights.

Roll up! Leap through!

Outside, beyond the neon tights, the paisley
sequinned flares of the artistes, tracing
such rococo knots in the canvas sky,
waits a lion called Frank, the last of his kind.
Tastes have changed, and lion-taming,
with such clear-cut rules of whip and chair,
has become passé, so yesterday.
The sententious prescripts of the pure—
that modern hygiene of the mind—
sweep scuddy sawdust aside like lice,
and draw a line through bear and lion.
So Frank, mane beige and moulting, lives
a most solitary life, a stuck record repeating
the rank smells of piss and popcorn,
the hooplah! and the swish of knives,
carving the air like a Sunday roast
around the tasty ribs of Madam Frisson.
She is just as bored and trapped as he
as she awaits her husband's swinging arm,
as sensitive as a brass metronome.
Soon Frank will be too shabby, even for this
ring of superannuated fantasy.
No scrubby savannah of reconciliation,
no release for a circus-bred beast,
into a sudden pride of compliance.
Just the screams from the audience
at the trapeze and the squirt-flowery gambit
of painted clown. His dreams are smeared
with a thin imagined relish of gazelle,
as he bobs and bobs that shameful mane.
Soon, though, the final bob; the final doze.
He'll leap, ungoaded, through the hoop of death
onto who knows what plains, what deer-rich grass?

music notes

piano accordion
the lung that smiles

haversack guts fart
sousaphone

less said the better
triangle

Jazz

Sax snaking
between notes,
tonguing air for directions,
poisonously honeyed
ears overflowing
quick thickening
and her voice,
both glacier and moraine
digging cool deep
graves of swoon,
lowering us in,
willingly, longingly
noise-swaddled
now punctuated by
exhortations of snare,
the metal finesse
of the cymbal
so jaggedly round
sweet clanging infraction
their fingers, her larynx
lynx swift yet subtle,
pouncing syncopation
delivers gasp-slaps
on listeners' lobes—
we clap pauseless poise

Guide to not writing haiku

Straining to create
seventeen syllable pups—
such stillborn haiku

13 words that should be in a poem

Tintinnabulate, with no little white dog.
Albedo, a lemon wedge of sun, no gin.
Froufrou whispering of salons most Prousty
Overheard by stuffy disapproving *frowzy*.
Bilby, because they're far better than rabbits.
Gubernatorial, before the Republic erupts!
Autochthonous ditto, when we ditch the Poms,
Just like the Indians, with bulk *pappadoms*.
Papillae and *papillote*, for nice soft curly fingers.
Isostasy threatened by two in that line I just writ.
Tectonic as panic rocks this poem's solidity,
But I pulled it together. Quite *sylleptically*.

Perfect words

Sometimes they reach out
caress with syllable fingers—
egregious is my long term love
half egret feathers with the jus
noise saucing the end,
despite the meaning
or because it's such a better way
to say doubleplusbad.

Gnarly enchants, with that
drowning g, wiping out
in the endless surf of the ee.
What wetsuit could protect,
what board shorts deserve
the sweet yet egregious sea,
with the tincture of shark grin
and the promise of release?

There are five poets in my garden

—and they think that they are bulbs.
But the first one smells carcinogenic,
and he is clothed in ancient brown,
as if he stole the mud-flecked jumper
from the very body of a bog-man.
The second is talking about
the fervid dangers of Pokémon,
and how in *her day*, they looked
for birds, and birds were quite enough.
She has a collection of empty eggs,
pilfered in *her day*, which lie
in an ancient purloined nest—
a weird eunuch's severed balls,
placed in a stolen cup of misery.
Number three is being thoughtful.
He never utters a sentence without
a French theorist's name—
like a pigeon (of stolen eggs) he says
Bourdieu, Bourdieu, and *oui*, he bores me.
Number four is addicted to rhyme.
He knows he is somewhat out of time,
but like a tune you know too well,
he is married to the villanelle.
And the fifth? She plants sarcasm
in a weedy succulent garden,
where such thin green tongues
poke like wee prickly dragons.
She's fully awesome, and awfully sweet.

Eighth in a long line of nasty little poems

Loud man pissing round the reading
with irrelevant comments,
dribbling self, reflected in a deep pool
of his own stewed past, steaming.
He is a true Narcissus,
but not so drop-dead gorgeous;
fungus mated with dead cat.
He smells of yesterday and loss.
He shouts his irrelevance
with every tedious joke,
every punch line a squib,
tarnishing the grey sky.

Second in a long series of nasty poems

A 'brilliant young man' from Sydney
Unfortunately ruptured a kidney —
For his black jeans won't zip
Round the tenure of hip,
Which perplexed our 'young' man from Sydney.

First in a long series of nasty little poems

She would surely
free the refugees —
but mostly those
with nice table manners.

Third in a long series of nasty little poems

Her stilettos so sharp
her brain the chewing gum
beneath one heel;
occasionally a thought sticks.

Outings

Out for review
Out for the count
Out of time
Out for lunch
Out and about
Out for a duck
Out of luck
Out of the closet
Out on the town
Out of the corner of my eye
Out of the box
Out of the mouths of babes
Out of fashion
Out caught behind
Out of it
Out and out
Over and out

(haiku 5)

Old men's ears
half lettuce and half slug
sprouting sound

(senryu 2)

Getting old —
I mix Laphroaig
with TISM

Twenty ways to keep your essentials to hand

Lucite pillbox flaunting small pearls
Shell shape clutch for pocket Venus
Curious net of cunning gold mesh
Eyebending sequins intricately sewn
Art deco black silk organically clasped
Ten thousand beaded fine French paisley
Quaint cigar box rolls lipsticks and tampons
Roomy Mexican holdall hammock wide
Oval pigskin (and it's not made by Sherrin)
Faux leopard snarls and real pony kicks
Kawaii Japanese anthropomorphic bear
Modest exquisite goldchained calf
Ironic grannysquared seventies repro
Tikis barkclothed for quick souvenirs
Crocodiles taught Parisian accents
Poodle pregnant with pompom coinpurse
Felt dubiously coloured and Etsyfied
Blue papoose flaunts fat fleshy handles
Concertina traincase bakelites makeup
Poet's tote with slant Dickinson quote

The poet contemplates the inescapable nature of the class system

A Richter moment of tectonic rock came
when I heard the voice of smug middle class
speaking through me. A mythic, conceited Volvo
blonde used me as her blank-eyed dummy,
stuck lovely manicure up me and made me say
'The guinea pigs don't like asparagus!'.
My ears could not believe my mouth's betrayal,
the change marked by that simple recipe.
The seesaw tipped, sudden rodeo bucking,
swung away from student furniture of bricks,
stray cushions and ideas, towards clogging
superannuation of risotto and good red.

Class catches us like butterflies, or half-frozen slugs,
which we pick, so carefully, from our organic greens.

I remember the lost skirt of Carlton

Nimble and nineteen, perhaps twenty, I saw you;
velvet A-line, satin belt, and my heart dropped open
knowing how you would swathe me in excellence
hang just right, soft as a crop of Labrador's dark ears.
Student poor, with a world to change, I stood outside,
longing, mental tongue lapping, dressed in thin dream.
Today, girt in husband's semi-silken wage,
(and the splendid coin of Poesie)
I could command your like be snipped
to the pattern of sweet memory.
But my waist has grown
along with his pay,
so perfect skirt, in time or space,
will always always
slip
away.

French police cut soles off migrant children's shoes

And some would say
the illegality would be to the property,
the abused ownership of the shoes,
not the feet, blistered by hope,
the minds, yearning; the law's barriers
are clear, clear as any fence.
Dubbed illegal, shoes truncated,
the children are sent *back* on trains.
Sole-less shoes are the new sans culottes,
as the French police cut the fashion.
And we, smug, tut-tut, and lock
the lame and the pregnant off-shore.
We cut the map, turn the sea into walls.
We are surgeons of souls, and watch,
as young men take the final step
and launch themselves, shoeless,
into another world, with hidden knife,
or rope, knot, and quick-flipped chair.

The poem's title derives from a headline in *The Guardian*, 15th June 2018: *https://www.theguardian.com/world/2018/jun/14/french-border-police-accused-of-cutting-soles-off-migrant-childrens-shoes*

Three first world concerns

The scholastic affliction—
virus transmits an urge
to write a PhD

Paleo or vegan diet?
Debate attracts more comments
than Palestine

American spelling triumphs—
well color me cheeks,
what's wrong with 'u'?

The canary, the pony, and the man

It sounds like a joke's first line,
a trio who walked into a bar.
But no, these are the three who
went below, swung down from the light.

One was there to pull loads
through dark roads carved
far from the sun, far from meadow,
half horse and half mole.

The bright bird, born for the sky,
would die first if the air was turning.
Now he is mere metaphor, cliché;
canary in the coal-mine has had his day.

Only the man still mines.
Each day he dives down to work,
amongst rich minerals and dust—
every day rising like Lazarus.

You can't stand outside

Those small hems of grass at the edge
of the pavement, skirting road and house—
nature strips, we call them.
As if nature were a thin green line
of easy demarcation,
a quaint decoration for real estate.
Long home to droops of grass,
and limp advertising leaflets,
spat from bored letterboxes
like soggy swear words,
promising a paradise of credit.
But now backs swell,
bums are fleshy pumpkins,
bending over to tend
your actual pumpkins.
Vegetable patches add a swatch
of nature to the nature strips,
cultivated as they may be.
They're small, these crops; pea small.
Peas placed under the mattress
of the market—hardly enough
to wake it from slumber.
That lazy princess dozes on,
dreaming the unseemly lives we live in.
And yet, as my neighbour said,
mulching with soggy leaflets—
if you can't stand outside things,
at least you can get outside

and grow a few things.
She turned her strong back,
tending to tumescent zucchinis,
and the impatient tomatoes
she will decant into twenty hungry jars.
She'll give some jars away,
or swap them for flowers or beans
in a cool, vegetable anarchy.

(Her recipe? Well, I would attach it,
but that's one thing she just won't share.)

The Princess shifts in her sleep.
The pumpkins are replete with seed.

Malcolm Turnbull's tie

Oh, when I curl up and die
please just let me be reborn
as Malcolm Turnbull's tie.

No-one could weep (or even sigh),
at the elegant prospect
of being hung as Malcolm's tie.

Way way way up on high
a spray-tanned face talks
above such a gorgeous tie.

And below that face lies
the endless, knotted glory
of a must-be imported tie.

We'd get on well, he and I,
as he smooths and flatters
above the silken tongue of tie.

So, when I curl up and die
please just let me be reborn
as Malcolm Turnbull's tie.

Faith took a holiday

He hitched down the Hume, or up;
he didn't tell me. Faith has no fear
of murder, or everyday sleazes
and their boring imprecations.
It's the ones left behind
who tend to fret. *What if,*
we say, and *perhaps...*
as if *perhaps* isn't Faith
flipped like a decisive coin,
standing on his head.
As if *as if* isn't
closer to *for sure*
than some might like it to be.

Faith rang me from Melbourne,
(so it was *down* the Hume)
and said he wanted to look around
a bit longer; catch the trams.
He too remembers
the excellent days of conductors,
with their magical brown bags.
Even Faith feels regret
at the passing of old days;
the spinning of so much
towards the expansive sun
of interconnected drivel.
There is a grace

in not knowing too much,
he said, though Faith would say that,
I suppose. That's his job.
A kind of conductor
unseen in any tram,
on any route, whatsoever.

Faith will return soon;
I can hear the jingling
just at the edge of thought
and the tune is one
I almost remember.
The brown bag of my
restless, overloaded brain
awaits his presence,
and will sling itself, eager,
over his patient arm.

Limits

Four months ago the trees looked like trees
drawn in charcoal by a depressed artist—
simple strokes of black connecting earth
to noon-time grey, throat-choking, skies.
Now, watch the festoons of green
circling the trunks, as if strewn
by the world's worst exterior decorator.
Such vivid newness, almost artificial
in its neon promise. And yet,

such trees have known blazes many years,
lightning-spat, or most carefully set,
by those who shaped the land,
farmed with fire, forty thousand years or more.
We comfort ourselves, forget that this mega-blaze,
man-made, was the very opposite of skill.
We have changed the seasons, charged
the air, dried the possibilities of rain
into a parched riverbed of loss.

Yes, the trees still push out leaves.
Frail canopy above dead mounds of wombat,
of lyre-bird-less, song-lost, ground.
The reassurance of regeneration
this time asks us how many more
times green can possibly appear.
If next year, and the next, another

blaze exceeds all history,
will even gumtrees stay gloomed —
dead sticks we poked into a lessened land?

Ten moments in the life of modern Jesus

1. At the bowls club, selling raffle tickets

2. Not voting for blustery Christians

3. Trying to eat vegetarian (locusts were never much chop)

4. Sipping light beer and saying it's just as good

5. Riding his bike (unless delivering meals)

6. Going Anglican to hear the chicks (vocational guidance systems lock on all sorts)

7. Walking the dogs on Canberra winter mornings (but not always picking up poo)

8. Buying The Big Issue *and reading it*

9. Studying obituary column poetry and not even thinking of laughing

10. Making sure that widows and widowers win the chook raffle (see 1 above) and sharing the meal (despite 3 above)

Except for the cat

The cancer riddled Staffie, the muzzle white where it was brindle once, the Great Dane who clocked up only three years (for we breed dogs too big for their strained hearts to cope), the smelly terrier who outlived them all, sitting with the bald budgie Chomp on his head (something that would never have been allowed when the dog was alive), the coin-sized islands of terrapin, the scurry of guinea pigs, the cat that adopted you even though you don't like cats, the many goldfish that floated to the tops of tanks, all come to greet you as you travel over to the other side. They bite and scratch and peck, and the ballooned goldfish push inside your throat, and you feel the choking although you are dead, and you realise that the animals did not enjoy their lives being stunted, to fit into your notion of *pet* like a blistered foot caught in a too small shoe. Except for the cat, who never gave a shit.

About the Author

PS Cottier has published seven books of poetry, a volume of stories, and a short non-fiction work describing the wildlife near Parliament House, called *Paths Into Inner Canberra* (Ginninderra Press, 2015). Her books have received commendations or prizes in a number of awards. She holds a Bachelor of Laws from the University of Melbourne and a PhD from the Australian National University, and has worked as a lawyer, tutor, union organiser and tea-lady.

PS Cottier is currently the Poetry Editor at The Canberra Times and a frequent book reviewer. She lives and writes on unceded Ngunnawal and Ngambri land.

Her blog is published at *pscottier.com*

www.ingramcontent.com/pod-product-compliance
Lightning Source LLC
Chambersburg PA
CBHW020328010526
44107CB00054B/2021